Scheduling To Improve Student Learning

Ron Williamson

National Middle School Association
Westerville, Ohio

Betty Edwards, Executive Director
Jeff Ward, Deputy Executive Director
April Tibbles, Director of Publications
Carla Weiland, Publications Editor
John Lounsbury, Editor, Professional Publications
Edward Brazee, Consulting Editor, Professional Publications
Mary Mitchell, Designer, Editorial Assistant
Dawn Williams, Publications Manager
Lindsay Kronmiller, Graphic Designer
Nikia Reveal, Graphic Designer
Marcia Meade-Hurst, Senior Publications Representative
Peggy Rajala, Marketing and Advertising Manager

Library of Congress Cataloging-in-Publication Data
Williamson, Ronald D.
  Scheduling to improve student learning/Ronald Williamson.
       p. cm.
  Includes bibliographical references.
  ISBN 978-1-56090-224-9
1. Schedules, School. 2. Middle schools--Administration. I. Title.
  LB3032.W55 2009
  373.12'42--dc22   2008046725

Dedication

To Ava, Ella, Lilly, and Owen, who have taught me about human growth and development and about the importance of high quality educational programs.

About the Author

Ron Williamson is currently professor of educational leadership at Eastern Michigan University. He was a middle school teacher, team leader, principal, and central office administrator in the Ann Arbor, Michigan, public schools for many years. A former executive director of National Middle School Association, Ron is the author or co-author of over 100 books, chapters, and articles about middle schools and school improvement. His work has appeared in all of the major middle level publications, including *Middle School Journal, NASSP Bulletin, Schools in the Middle,* and *School Administrator*. Ron was awarded the Gruhn-Long-Melton award in recognition of lifetime achievement in middle level leadership. He works extensively with secondary schools throughout the nation as a program evaluator, assessment consultant, and specialist in the design of school schedules.

Contents

1

Starting the Scheduling Conversation

Principals work in one of the most complex and challenging environments imaginable. Expected to provide a quality educational experience for each of their students in an era of high accountability, to balance the competing demands of parent and community groups with the needs of students, and to be knowledgeable experts about curriculum and instruction, they must at the same time manage the day-to-day functions of their schools. Principals must lead in providing a rich and engaging instructional program that is built and sustained on nurturing and caring relationships among students, teachers, and other school personnel.

The professional literature tells us these meaningful relationships, so essential to the learning environment, are an outcome of learning communities built on a foundation of interdisciplinary teams. While the models for teaming vary in size and emphasis, most middle school interdisciplinary teams are comprised of two to five teachers who have primary responsibility for instructing a group of students in the basic academic areas. Teaming is the hallmark of a good middle school, and when effectively implemented, it positively impacts student learning and the school climate.

One of the forces driving the adoption of teaming is the recognition that when teachers collaborate, they can increase their effectiveness in fostering student learning by using a variety of instructional practices especially appropriate for young adolescents, ones that engage them intellectually and often physically as well. Essential to the use of these practices is a schedule that provides sufficient time for these more extensive strategies. Teams cannot achieve their full potential unless the schedule and other school structures are also modified. As a result, middle school educators have developed a variety of scheduling models to provide teachers and teams with a longer instructional block.

The importance of a shared vision

This book will discuss several important lessons learned by principals who have changed their schools' structures. Perhaps the most important lesson is that organizational patterns must be guided by clearly articulated and accepted goals. A quality schedule emerges only when teachers and administrators have worked together designing it— and that design is guided by a shared vision. Without common goals, the school schedule is merely an administrative plan for organizing teachers and students into groups. When guided by identified goals, however, the schedule becomes a powerful tool to positively impact teaching and learning.

The experience of a school in northern Ohio illustrates the importance of goals. For several years the faculty sought a way to "change the schedule." They discussed options, visited other schools, and debated the merits of alternative designs. Never did they talk directly about what they wanted to accomplish with a new schedule.

During the past year the staff returned to the question of a new schedule. This time, however, they spent considerable time discussing why they wanted to change, what they wanted to achieve, and why a change would benefit students. Two critical goals emerged from the discussion—longer instructional blocks for each class and common planning time for teachers in their teams. Guided by these specific goals, a faculty committee quickly narrowed the schedule options and developed several alternatives from which the staff selected a "new" schedule.

In a seminal book on middle schools, *Successful Schools for Young Adolescents*, Joan Lipsitz (1984) described the programs of four successful middle schools. Her analysis noted that while each school used a different organizational model, in every case the schedule was driven by the school's philosophy. While the schedule varied, each school's commitment to aligning its organizational model with the needs of students was a defining characteristic and was the single most important factor in selecting the model.

Factors affecting developmentally responsive schedules

In *This We Believe: Successful Schools for Young Adolescents* (2003), National Middle School Association outlined 14 attributes of successful middle schools. While all 14 of these interrelated characteristics indirectly impact curriculum and instruction, the following four are particularly relevant to scheduling:

- Students and teachers that engage in active learning.
- Curriculum that is relevant, challenging, integrative, and exploratory.
- Multiple learning and teaching approaches that respond to their diversity.
- Organizational structures that support meaningful relationships and learning. (p. 7)

In addition, other professional groups such as National Association of Secondary School Principals (NASSP) and the National Forum to Accelerate Middle-Grades Reform have visions of high-performing middle level schools that are rooted in creating personalized environments that can meet the developmental needs of young adolescents. Scheduling is an essential component of providing smaller learning environments in which teachers know their students on personal levels. A more accurate picture is painted of each student as multiple perspectives emerge from meetings when teams discuss their students and plan ways to support their ever-changing development.

As preparation for standardized tests has increased in importance, it has taken up more of the schedule, while time for classes such as physical education and even social studies and science have been reduced. Some considerations, not always subject-specific, that need to be kept in mind as a school considers reconfiguring its schedule are

- Time for students to actively participate in transitioning from observing the concrete world to establishing relationships and reflecting on their experiences.
- Time for weighing options and making choices and decisions that will deepen students' abilities to reason and increase the responsibility they feel for their educations.
- Time for forming connections among subjects so young adolescents can understand the interrelatedness of what they are learning.
- Time for health and physical education experiences critical for young adolescents' establishing the lifestyle habits and choices that will help them negotiate the awkward times when their bodies are taking shape.
- Time for providing forums and related information sessions so students can understand the nature and consequences of risky behaviors and minimize the likelihood of developing unhealthy habits.
- Time for experiences that will help young adolescents struggling with the many choices, decisions, relationships, and identity issues involved in their social and moral development.

- Time for opening to all students programs such as conflict management and peer mediation that put them in meaningful roles and help them feel connected.
- Time for exploring new areas of study that respond to their heightened curiosity.

All of these considerations, as well as many others, have clear scheduling implications, making the job of developing a balanced schedule a real challenge.

The concept of developmental responsiveness, which is central to the middle school movement, has often been misunderstood. Critics of the middle school suggest that it creates a climate in which attention to intellectual development is secondary to issues of self-esteem. Nothing could be further from the truth! When reporting on the intent of middle school advocates, such leaders as Dickinson (2001) and Jackson and Davis (2000) assert that middle grades schools are places where intellectual development is central. The National Forum's criteria for successful middle grades schools also reflect the primacy of academic excellence. Middle level educators, cognizant of the developmental characteristics of 10- to 15-year-olds, know the many developmental changes that young adolescents experience often have a priority in their daily lives. Therefore, it is necessary for the school to help meet those developmental needs in order to effectively meet its primary academic responsibility.

Scheduling options

There are four primary ways to provide some flexibility in the schedule: the block schedule, the alternating schedule, the rotating schedule, and the dropped schedule.

A block schedule creates longer instructional periods, called blocks, while an alternating schedule varies the schedule from day to day or semester to semester. The most common rotating model literally rotates the placement of classes from day to day, so that classes meet at different times. Finally, a dropped schedule drops one or two classes occasionally to allow a place for student clubs or other activities to meet during the school day.

While each of these alternatives to the traditional schedule has some merit, the model most frequently found in middle schools is the block schedule that supports interdisciplinary teaming and other middle school goals. Hackmann and Valentine (1998) claim, "the worth of interdisciplinary teaming has been so thoroughly documented that the issue has become a 'given' when speaking of organizational expectations of a quality middle level program" (p. 1). Accumulating experience and research studies do show that when teachers, individually or as a team, have longer instructional blocks, they modify their instructional practice, use more engaging hands-on activities, conduct deeper discussions of key concepts, and give students sufficient time to reflect on and make meaning of their learning.

Benefits of a block schedule

A block schedule, regardless of the particular model used, provides longer periods of instructional time than does a traditional fixed period-by-period schedule. This increased class time allows teachers to vary the format of their classes. Meri Kock, an eighth grade math teacher, found the block schedule expanded her educational repertoire.

> Having the block time allows me to have the students conduct an experiment, take measurements, play mathematical games, collect data, and then analyze what we've done while everything is still fresh in their minds. If the students want to explore some aspect of an activity further, I know I can take off in that direction with them without having to watch the clock or worry about the bell interrupting us. (Gallagher, 1999, p. 10)

Out-of-class activities, such as a nature walk or a field trip can be carried out in the longer block. Debates, Socratic seminars, mock trials, and cooperative learning activities are among the types of activities that work best in a block. Its flexibility allows teachers to conduct a wide selection of instructional strategies. No longer compelled to select approaches that fit within 45–50 minutes, teachers can choose instructional practices that tap their creativity and capitalize on the energy of students.

In addition to the potential instructional benefits, schools that implement longer instructional blocks frequently see a positive impact on school climate. There are often fewer class changes, resulting in fewer hallway incidents, and stress for both students and teachers seems to be reduced.

Longer instructional blocks, when implemented as part of teaming, provide still additional benefits. Teachers forge real connections with their colleagues as they discuss ways to connect their content areas and share instructional strategies.

Lessons from other schools

Those principals who are most successful in changing their schools' schedules are inevitably ones who work closely with their teachers. They value the suggestions of their staffs, view them as collaborators, and respect the varied points of view expressed. From such principals several important lessons emerged.

Start with clearly identified goals.

Rarely is a school successful in improving instruction when it simply changes the schedule to change the schedule. A thorough discussion of the benefits and goals of changing the schedule not only builds support for the new model, but also narrows the alternatives that might be selected. Full discussion provides an opportunity to build consensus for the initiative and allows faculty members less eager for change to participate in the discussion and have their concerns addressed. Examples of questions a principal might use to guide a discussion of goals are

- What do we want to achieve with a modified schedule?
- Do some subjects need more time than others?
- Do all classes need to meet each day?
- Do we want to facilitate curriculum integration?
- How can we allocate time based on the needs of our students?

Challenge long-standing norms.

Principals can challenge long-standing assumptions and norms about the schedule that has come to provide structure, stability, and security for the faculty. In western New York, for instance, one principal found that most of his staff believed their current schedule was necessary due to the state requirements for minutes of instruction in specific content areas. Even when shown a copy of the state requirements, many staff continued to insist that the principal was incorrect and had faulty information. He persevered in confronting these long-held but erroneous beliefs, which ultimately led to a productive discussion about creating longer instructional blocks.

A principal from Colorado conducted a short, anonymous survey of his staff about their current schedule and alternatives. When the issue was first raised at staff meetings, a few vocal teachers opposing change always said, "Nobody wants to change what we have. Our current schedule works." Others who supported a change were reluctant to confront these teachers. The survey results demonstrated overwhelming support for modifying the schedule. These data transformed the tone of the conversation among the faculty.

Collaborate to identify values.

Change is most successful, of course, when it is broadly supported among the faculty. Imposing a schedule and insisting on a different model will create resistance. A study of school reform, not surprisingly, found that distributed leadership characterized the most successful cases. Teachers as well as administrators shared responsibility for charting the course of instructional improvement, for articulating the benefits of a modified program, and for selecting strategies appropriate for their schools (Murphy & Datnow, 2003).

A principal in southeastern Michigan described the importance of working with his staff in these words:

> In the beginning most teachers thought scheduling was easy. Just move a few classes they thought. Boy were they surprised. They learned how complex the process is, how everything in the schedule is connected to everything else. By allowing them to realize the complexity of adjusting the schedule and all the factors that must be considered, we ended up with broader support. Teachers talked with other teachers and explained why our new model would work, and why we selected this option. It wouldn't have been the same if I had done it alone.

Besides building support, participation in planning serves as an important form of professional development. When teachers are involved in investigating scheduling options, learning about their benefits, and recommending a model, they are engaged in meaningful professional development.

Assure a balanced review.

When launching an initiative to change the schedule, the principal must assure that both advantages and disadvantages of each option are discussed. Because there are no perfect schedules, every option has benefits and costs. Open, honest discussion of each alternative builds support for the one selected. One California principal said, "If I tried to ram it through and not have a balanced discussion, it would haunt me in the end. So, let's talk about it openly and make a decision based on a both the advantages and disadvantages."

Concluding thoughts

The flexibility that longer instructional blocks provide is a critical condition for improving the quality of teaching and learning. Blocks allow greater variety of instruction activities, provide for more hands-on activities, improve school climate, and build a heightened sense of connectedness among teachers, students, and curricular areas.

While the benefits of the block are clear, it is also clear that schools are most successful in moving to the model when the decision is based on a clear set of goals, a thorough examination of the alternatives, discussion of both advantages and disadvantages of each alternative, and a shared commitment to improving the educational experience of all students.

References

Dickinson, T. (Ed.) (2001). *Reinventing the middle school.* New York: Routledge Falmer.

Gallagher, J. (1999). Teaching in the block. *Middle Ground, 2*(3), 12.

Hackmann, D., & Valentine, J. (1998). Designing an effective middle level schedule. *Middle School Journal, 29*(5), 1.

Jackson, A., & Davis, G. (2000). *Turning Points 2000: Educating adolescents in the 21st century.* New York: Teachers College Press.

Lipsitz, J. (1984). *Successful schools for young adolescents.* New York: Transaction Books.

Murphy, J., & Datnow, A. (2003). *Leadership lessons from comprehensive school reforms.* Thousand Oaks, CA: Corwin Press.

National Middle School Association. (2003). *This we believe: Successful schools for young adolescents.* Westerville, OH: Author.

2

Focusing on Instructional Change

Let's be clear on what changing your school schedule will and will not do. Changing the school schedule will *not*

- Automatically change the way teachers teach.
- Remove barriers such as bus schedules, physical plant limitations, and contractual conditions.
- Result in major curricular and instructional change.
- Alter the demographics of the student body.

Your school schedule should be based on your school philosophy and vision; so if your school is in need of instructional change, a foundation must first be laid that will fit your schedule.

The need for change

A middle level principal recently remarked, "I just can't seem to get the staff to change the way they teach. Most of them have been teaching for years, and they're not excited about changing their ways."

This principal's dilemma illustrates a growing concern throughout the nation—the ability of teachers to address the needs of an increasingly diverse student body. Educators have become sensitive to the changing demographics of students and their families: increased ethnic diversity, greater range of socioeconomic factors, more single-parent families, and the predominance of households where both parents work.

At the same time that the demographics of American classrooms changed, educators developed a better understanding of the varied ways students learn. Along with improved understanding about how students learn, several researchers have advanced concepts or approaches that will respond to the diverse nature and needs of adolescents. They include Marzano's *Building*

Background Knowledge for Academic Achievement: Research on What Works in Schools (2004); Johnson and Johnson's, *Leading the Cooperative School* (1989); and Gardner's *The Theory of Multiple Intelligences* (1983). Each reflects an appreciation for a range of learning styles and modalities.

How do you begin?

While some teachers became increasingly responsive, many others failed to embrace changes in their practices. One principal remarked: "I've sent them to conferences. We've had training on site. Yet, when I visit classrooms I see little difference in what's going on. What can I do?"

During a recent study of instructional practices in middle levels schools principals shared their experiences with this issue. The stories of their successes offer a menu of strategies to guide the efforts of other middle level schools as they strengthen their instructional programs, first by collaboratively creating a climate for change, then by identifying a learning community philosophy, and finally, by creating a schedule to bring the process to fruition.

1. Create a climate receptive to change.

Following are two strategies principals have used successfully to increase their staffs' openness to change.

Learning styles approach: One approach used by many principals was to raise staff awareness of their own diversity. Several principals devoted a faculty meeting or a portion of a staff development day to use a learning styles instrument such as True Colors Personality Test or Myers-Briggs-Type Indicator (see www.truecolorspersonalitytest.com and http://www.myersbriggs.org).

A benefit of this approach was that as staff became more sensitive to their own range of working styles, they transferred their learning about themselves to their work with students—to their own teaching and learning practices. In one southern middle school the principal asked his teachers to meet in "style similar" groups and respond to a series of questions (e.g., What are the conditions for your best work? What causes you stress and frustration?).

As they responded, the teachers grappled with their own learning styles and began to recognize the importance of allowing for a variety of styles. Following the initial work, the principal invited each group to share its discussion. The groups expressed startlingly different needs, which led to a conversation about how these insights could impact their work with students.

The principal then asked staff to work in "style different" groups. Their new task was to "describe the look and feel of interaction when working with other adults." This and other tasks provoked rich discussion. In describing the results, the principal reported, "Teachers discovered that they were not all alike—the needs of some teachers were dramatically different from others. It had a profound impact on the way we work with one another."

Pros and cons approach: In a midwestern school the principal asked faculty to imagine that they were about to undertake a major restructuring project. He invited them to describe the conditions under which "they would be willing to support and commit to the new initiative" and to "indicate any special needs" they had regarding the presentation of material, exploration of alternatives, and decision-making processes.

As expected, a large number of ideas were received, many quite different. Based on the responses, the principal charted a course of action that would both meet the needs of faculty and minimize the anxiety associated with the project. What emerged was a plan that incorporated several activities—each meeting the needs of a distinct group of faculty.

One group described itself as interested in what the research says and established a study group to review a number of approaches, to discuss the theories and investigate the results of research. A second group, less concerned about research, was passionately interested in the impact of any change on the people involved. Their interest in the "human-dimension" led them to develop a survey of staff about the types of resources required for changing instructional practice. They wanted to assure that individuals felt supported. Yet another group was interested in the organization and logistics of the project and developed a tentative time line and plan for moving forward, including detailed steps and decision points.

About two months into the project, the principal devoted one faculty meeting to debriefing. There was general agreement that approaching the task from a variety of ways met not only the needs of individuals but also those of the total group. The tasks complemented one another and contributed to the overall success of the project. He reported based on this experience, that the faculty is more receptive to refining their instructional practice. "They came to appreciate tailoring the activity to their interests," he stated, "but more than that many of my teachers are now talking about how they can use such an approach in their own classrooms. Now that's progress!"

The experience of these principals illustrates the impact of a leader. They engaged teachers in activities that raised their sensitivity to differences in working and learning styles. They involved staff in planning activities that responded to their unique styles and needs. They quietly and unobtrusively established a climate that was receptive to examining teaching and learning processes, which would eventually lead to making critical scheduling decisions.

2. Identify limiting factors.
Even when teachers fully realize that the current schedule does limit what teachers and students can accomplish, rationale for maintaining the status quo can come from many directions.

- Comfort and familiarity with the current schedule.
- Belief that the change is too extensive.
- Belief that the change would require considerable teacher training.
- Parents could object.

And quite often, underlying the stated rationales is that unspoken but very real fear many teachers have, that they are not personally able to handle the innovation. Prior to starting a conversation about significant changes to the school schedule, it is important to recognize such factors and be ready to counter them.

3. Create a common vision.
No factor is of greater importance than the vision that teachers and administrators hold for their school. Without a clear vision, the schedule, by itself, will make little difference in the educational experience of students.

A major misconception about schedules is that adopting a different scheduling model will result in major curricular and instructional change. This teacher comment often follows adoption of a new schedule. "I thought things would be different, but nothing seems to have changed." But when a schedule that is based on shared beliefs and a common vision is created, teachers and other personnel will make it work for the betterment of students.

4. Be clear about priorities
It is possible to schedule almost anything. The dilemma is that school personnel have competing priorities, priorities that cannot be accommodated in the same schedule. All a school's goals cannot be fully achieved through a single schedule. Therefore, as important as having a shared vision is the

importance of having clear priorities. Priorities—what is most important to accomplish—help to sort through the advantages and disadvantages of potential schedules.

One example of the process of reaching a shared vision comes from the staff at a school in suburban Pittsburgh who wanted to change the schedule to provide long instructional blocks for teaching teams. A study group convened to examine the options and make a recommendation.

Shortly after the group began its work, it became apparent that individual members held quite different opinions about what should be accomplished. For example, some teachers believed every team should have an instructional block of at least three consecutive class periods. Others wanted only shorter blocks. Still other teachers wanted students' two exploratory classes scheduled back-to-back.

Clearly not all of the priorities could be achieved in the same schedule. After listing all of the suggestions, the group discussed each one. The goal was to understand the suggestion and to clarify the implications. Through these conversations the group generated a list of their common priorities. As often happens, the final list balanced the competing desires. The final list of priorities stated that all instructional blocks would be at least 90 minutes long, the priority for the longest blocks would be with the sixth grade, and the two exploratory classes would be scheduled back-to-back in at least one of the three grades.

Identifying priorities prior to designing a schedule provides an opportunity to develop a schedule that will address the identified needs. Otherwise, priorities may be met only "by chance," leading to frustration for those involved. Identifying priorities early can significantly impact the final schedule design.

5. Gather and use data
School personnel are inundated with data—data about student achievement, demographics, absenteeism, suspension, and more—but they aren't always used in making decisions. Data are essential when considering a new schedule. There are several ways that important information can be secured for use in scheduling decisions.

Surveys—Conducting a short survey of all staff about scheduling priorities provides an opportunity for everyone to be involved initially in providing input to the schedule.

Student learning data—These data include results on state or local assessments of student learning and often reveal significant information. For example, one district in Illinois carefully reviewed test results and found that students at all grade levels, especially when looking at identified subgroups, consistently under-performed in reading, language arts, and mathematics. These data were complemented by information about state expectations and sanctions. This led to a discussion about how to provide additional time for these content areas, which emerged as a priority for the school's new schedule.

Current use of time—The allocation of time in a school's schedule often remains the same from year to year. The only thing that may change is a shifting of subjects from one class period to another. Rarely do school personnel conduct a fundamental study of their current practices. One school, as part of designing a new schedule, chose to look closely at current time allocation as shown in the chart.

Category	Time (minutes)
Core Classes (math, science, language arts, social studies)	180 (4 x 45)
Exploratory Classes	135 (3 x 45)
Lunch	30
Passing Time	35
Homeroom	30

The study group realized that only 44% of the school day was committed to core subjects (mathematics, science, language arts, social studies) with other activities consuming 56% of the day.

These data changed the conversation. Rather than debate how to juggle the current activities, the study group discussed whether or not the allocation of time in the current schedule was appropriate. They examined the required curriculum and reviewed a test-item analysis of the most recent student learning data. As a result, they decided that any new schedule must provide additional time for reading or language arts and mathematics. Data focused and altered the conversation.

6. Model values.

Modeling is the most powerful tool a leader has to direct and shape school life. Every conversation, every action, every decision serves as a potent signal about what is prized and valued. Below are three strategies that middle level principals used to model effective practices. In each case, the principal selected approaches that incorporated current research on varied learning and working styles.

Bloom's Taxonomy strategy: A middle school in the southeast committed to greater use of Bloom's Taxonomy as an instructional tool. Following early deliberations, teachers predicted it would never be mentioned again and would be impossible to add to their workload anyway. Quietly and without fanfare, the principal responded by using Bloom's Taxonomy as a tool in her interaction with staff. Rather than relying solely on the lowest levels (knowledge and understanding), she began to pose questions and suggest activities that incorporated the higher levels (analysis, synthesis, evaluation). For example, rather than asking staff to provide a list of items required for the start of the new school year, she asked that they critique past start-ups (evaluations) and develop a set of recommendations for improvement (synthesis).

The taxonomy was used for other interactions as well. When speaking with staff, she carefully chose language that required higher-level thinking. When working with groups, she structured the task to incorporate a range of Bloom's levels. Each and every task was carefully crafted to model the use of higher level thinking skills. At a subsequent staff meeting the principal asked the staff to critique her efforts. The discussion revealed a subtle shift in the staff's appreciation of such tools. Together they began to generate a menu of approaches that could be used to transfer their appreciation to classrooms.

Multiple intelligences strategy: Another example of a principal's modeling values occurred in a midwestern school trying to use Gardner's theory of multiple intelligences (1983) to enhance its program. The principal, seizing the opportunity, made a subtle change in the format of faculty meetings. Building on the theory, he structured the meetings so that faculty could interact with one another (interpersonal), used role-playing when discussing topics such as dealing with an angry parent (bodily-kinesthetic), told stories or anecdotes to illustrate concepts (linguistic), and used Socratic questioning with statistics and data to illustrate points (logical-mathematical). The importance of the changes is illustrated in his comments, "After a while people caught on to what I was doing. It almost became a game—figure out the intelligence I was using. But this effort launched us to a new level. We began to regularly and routinely talk about instruction and ways to better serve kids."

Evaluation systems strategy: Yet another principal shared her experience using the evaluation system as a way to model the importance of instructional responsiveness. Her school used standard evaluation procedures—observations, conferences, and completion of checklists. Past practice was to observe and, in the absence of any major problems, hold a short conference prior to finalizing the form. In a startling departure the principal began to engage teachers in more thoughtful and reflective conferences. She spoke about her experience:

> When I began asking questions about student learning, about what they thought about when making decisions about their teaching, about how they used knowledge of student learning to shape their lessons, the climate changed. Teachers became much more attentive to using what they knew about student learning styles and multiple intelligences. I was amazed at the impact of those simple questions. Teachers really enjoyed the chance to talk about their teaching.

The principals using these strategies discovered that by rethinking the way they dealt with various school responsibilities—correspondence, faculty meetings, and evaluation conferences—they were able to positively impact their schools' instructional programs. Their modeling served in a very tangible way to demonstrate the importance placed on responsiveness to student learning styles.

7. Capitalize on school culture
Understanding culture allows school leaders to use it as a tool in modifying their programs. The importance of culture is described this way:

> Culture is a social invention created to give meaning to human endeavor. It provides stability, certainty, and predictability. People fear ambiguity and want assurance that they are in control of their surroundings. Culture imbues life with meaning and through symbols creates a sense of efficacy and control. (Deal & Kennedy, 1982, p. 7)

Understanding culture is not easy. An amorphous concept, culture becomes tangible when certain indicators such as core values, heroes, rites, rituals, stories, and conversations are examined. Values, the basic concepts and beliefs of an organization, are central to all institutions, and organizations with strong cultures are those in which the leaders articulate their beliefs openly and effectively. Organizational values are transmitted both formally and informally.

One other indicator of culture is made up of stories and conversations, formal and informal communications that transmit cultural values. This network formed, in part, by those inside the organization conveys stories about the organization. These stories often express, through anecdotes and tales, the organization's most prized values. Leaders are able to shape the culture of their schools through the stories they tell, the heroes and heroines they recognize, and the rites and rituals they establish. Several principals described how they used these cultural attributes to change the attitude in their schools toward instructional change.

Refocus "old stories": When he moved to a new school, a principal was confronted by a procession of teachers and parents who described problems at the school. Most stories focused on serious incidents with students or unresponsive teachers. Seizing the opportunity, the principal identified students who succeeded in the face of overwhelming odds, teachers who engaged in creative and innovative teaching, and parents most committed to the school's success. He used every opportunity to share their stories with faculty, with parent organizations, at community service meetings, following church, and at the post office and grocery store. As a result he found that, while the "old stories" continued to circulate to a degree, teachers and parents started to perceive the school differently.

Teachers as heroes and heroines: Another principal changed her school's use of staff development. Prior to her arrival, staff development meant "listening to a speaker, taking a few notes, and making few changes." She convened the School Improvement Council and asked members to help her design an alternative approach. With the council's support, a model emerged showcasing teachers as experts—sharing their instructional innovations, discussing their successes and failures, and posing critical instructional questions. By changing the ritual of staff development and making heroes and heroines of innovative teachers, this principal used culture to strengthen her school's program.

Concluding thoughts

Middle level educators recognize the need to respond to the diverse learning styles of students. The schedule and the process of changing it are two tools that help to meet these needs. In the face of increasing diversity, the challenge for leaders remains the same: to encourage and support their teachers' use of instructional practices that reflect a range of learning styles and promote success among all students.

Principals play a critical role in shaping their schools' programs. By embracing greater responsiveness to diverse student learning needs and capitalizing on the schedule as a means of offering support, principals can create a school environment that nurtures and supports instructional innovation and high student achievement.

References

Deal, T., & Kennedy, A. (1982). *Corporate cultures: The rites and rituals of corporate life.* Reading, MA: Addison-Wesley.

Gardner, H. (1983). *Frames of mind: The theory of multiple intelligences.* New York: Basic Books.

Johnson D., & Johnson, R. (1989). *Leading the cooperative school.* Edina, MN: Interaction Book Company.

Marzano, R. (2004). *Building background knowledge for academic achievement: Research on what works in schools.* Alexandria, VA: Association for Supervision and Curriculum Development.

3

Breaking the Mold

A rite of spring in every middle level school is planning the schedule for the following year. Mention of this activity prompts thoughts of singletons, doubletons, conflict matrices, and stacks of student course selections for school administrators to sort. In addition, teachers begin lobbying for select classes and preferred planning time. Thus begins the quest for the "ideal" master schedule.

Time as a resource

As schools continue their quest for an ideal schedule, it is important to maintain a perspective on the scheduling process. Hundreds, indeed thousands, of good schedules exist, but there is no perfect one. Each schedule reflects the unique characteristics and resources of its own school community and the philosophies of its faculty and administration. Each establishes a framework within which teachers, for the most part, are comfortable.

In *Successful Schools for Young Adolescents*, Joan Lipsitz (1984) described the programs of four successful middle level schools, each within a different organizational model. Each model evolved over time, and none of the schools were completely satisfied with their current model. She summarized the schools' efforts:

> The lesson about structure is seen in words like organic and evolving. The principals had a vision of what schooling should be like for young adolescents that did not start with teams or houses. Organizational decisions resulted from school philosophy. School philosophy was deeply influenced by sensitivity to the age group. It was also influenced by the personalities of talented leaders and a core group of highly dedicated teachers responding to the clamorous demands of a group of students whose energies they enjoy and wish to promote. (p. 193)

Creative and flexible use of time must become the norm as teachers and principals find ways to respond organizationally to their commitment to young adolescents. Four attributes emerge from schools that view time as a resource rather than a barrier. First, those schools use a variety of organizational arrangements to gain flexibility, which is not linked solely to interdisciplinary teams. Second, teachers in such schools are empowered to make decisions regarding the use of time. Third, a premium is placed on flexibility and responsiveness in the schools' routines; and finally, these schools modify their curricular and instructional practice, taking advantage of the options their schedules provide.

Challenging orthodoxy

"Research shows that effective teams lead to improved student achievement, increased parental contacts, an enhanced school climate, and positive student attitudes" (National Middle School Association, 2003, p. 29). Using teams moves curricular and instructional decisions closer to students, and teachers laud their own abilities to make decisions about grouping, instructional strategies, curriculum, and time allotments. Studies show a rise in the use of interdisciplinary teams as an organizational arrangement for the core curriculum faculty, and teaming is now majority practice in middle level schools (McEwin, Dickinson, & Jenkins, 2004; Valentine, Clark, Hackmann & Petzko, 2002). However, it is quite evident that even in many middle schools that are organized by teams, departmentalized instruction prevails.

Teaming gives teachers flexibility and the chance to collaborate. They can modify the way time is used to accommodate special projects and activities. Of course, a team may choose to maintain a traditional schedule of separate fixed-length class periods, while only occasionally venturing out to conduct an interdisciplinary unit.

Too often emphasis has been placed on the organizational elements of teaming and block scheduling. Principals and teachers have struggled with decisions about the number of team members, the amount of planning time, the length of instructional blocks, and ways of tracking team decisions. These "inputs" often facilitate the discussion but too frequently become ends rather than means.

The struggle for the perfect schedule often distracts middle level educators from the important task of finding ways to build flexibility into the school day, to respond appropriately to young adolescents, and to see time as a resource to be used. Educators must shift from implementing prescribed "inputs" to using various engaging approaches that will ensure critical "outputs" for young adolescents.

Making such a shift requires that educators challenge the orthodoxy of most schools. Orthodoxy is reflected in an absolute devotion to prescribed practices and accepted rituals. Increasingly, educators recognize that there is no one best model or correct approach for educating young adolescents. Challenging the orthodoxy around schedules frees teachers and principals to think broadly and explore a range of organizational options for using time.

A range of organizational arrangements

Many schools have used practices that provide flexibility. A school in Arizona organized teams of various sizes and configurations. Some teams have two teachers, others four. Some teams stay together for more than one year, others change every year. A school in Michigan offers both a departmental-based program and an interdisciplinary team option, with students and parents selecting the program they prefer.

Other organizational arrangements emerged. One school in Ohio adopted the school-within-a-school model by creating three small houses to serve nearly 1,000 students. Each house of 333 students was comprised of three teams—one sixth, one seventh, and one eighth—and each house occupied a separate floor of the school. While the students have different teachers each year, they remained part of the same house for all three years.

Such organizational arrangements provide a structure in which teachers and students can use their time more effectively and efficiently. It enhances interdisciplinary contacts, provides options for multi-grade groupings, and allows for easier modification of the daily schedule. These more innovative models are discussed in Chapter 5.

There are several ways to structure the school schedule to provide flexibility other than the team-based block-of-time schedule. They include large blocked classes (Carroll, 1989), the four-block semester plan (Edwards, 1993), the eight-block alternating day schedule (Hackmann, 1995), as well as rotating schedules and dropped schedules (Williamson, 1998) that are discussed later.

Any model has both advantages and disadvantages and should be evaluated based upon the particular set of circumstances in a school community. Factors to be considered include: traditional expectations, the school's philosophy, resources available, receptivity of faculty and parents, and facilities. Among desired conditions to be considered in a flexible schedule are these:

- Ability to vary the length of time allotted to individual subjects or classes based upon teacher and student need.
- Opportunities to conduct special activities—assemblies, team meetings, field trips—without disrupting the entire day or all staff.
- Opportunities to group and regroup students without totally reorganizing classes or tracking.
- Opportunities to integrate the curriculum.
- Options for both large- and small-group instruction.

At one midwestern middle level school, an eighth grade team was concerned about student behavior and attitude. The team had a four-hour block from 8:00 a.m. until noon. During that time students rotated among the four teachers. After lengthy discussion the team decided to rotate the groups throughout the year. For one group of students this meant that in September they went to science first, followed by math, social studies, and language arts. Beginning in October the rotation changed to math, social studies, language arts, and then science. In November it was social studies, language arts, science, and math. Every month of the year the schedule rotated.

Both teachers and students raved about this arrangement. Teachers who previously had seen students just before lunch discovered that the students were quite different first thing in the morning. The rotated schedule provided fresh perspectives for both students and teachers and provided a more balanced approach to teaching and learning in each area.

Instructional activities supported by a flexible schedule

Changing organizational arrangements and building flexibility into a school's schedule only creates the *potential* for curricular and instructional improvement, but with a block of time at their disposal, almost inevitably teachers move toward creating more of a laboratory for what was mainly a lecture hall. Some of the instructional strategies or activities that are possible in the larger block are these:

- *Projects that involve creating, painting, building, and making* some product or artifact.
- *Large or small-group instruction* that calls for regrouping students at intervals.

- *Interdisciplinary or thematic units* that involve some co-teaching and engaging activities.
- *Service learning projects*, preferably parts of an academic study, that get students out into the community.
- *Laboratory-type activities* such as science experiments that can be set up, conducted, and discussed in a longer period. Writing labs, simulations, and debates likewise work best in extended periods.
- *Guest speakers* who meet with all students at once and have time for questions and answers.
- *Learning stations* that call for students to work their way through a number of stations, either as individuals or as small groups.
- *Assemblies* that allow school, team, or grade-level events to be scheduled during the block.
- *Unit culminating activities* allow students to demonstrate and share their learnings with others.
- *Field trips and other out-of-the-building experiences*, which can often be completed without disrupting other classes.
- *Team meetings* that allow time for planning a project, sharing a special activity, or celebrating achievements—all important happenings in a learning community.

Rooms in which such activities take place provide students with a rich curriculum in which they use written and oral communication in functional contexts. Those rooms, more nearly workrooms than classrooms, require students to do more than just store and retrieve information; they analyze, synthesize, and evaluate information and ideas, and they engage in critical thinking and productive problem solving.

Empower teachers to make decisions

Schools that regard time as a resource also place importance on empowering teachers to make decisions about its use. A recent study of effective middle level schools in Michigan found that principals of schools that successfully implemented interdisciplinary teaming had empowered their teachers to make scheduling decisions. For example, in one school a team of eighth grade teachers collaboratively decided to alter the schedules within their team of a group of students experiencing problems. Once the mix of students was changed, the work of the students improved, and they were more positive about team activities. The team leader described the importance of being empowered to make such decisions: "The team was able to identify the problem, discuss options, and make a decision to resolve the problem."

Another example of teachers empowered to make schedule decisions was a seventh grade team who modified the swimming schedule. Rather than swimming every other day for two weeks, the students swam two hours on four consecutive days, thus saving travel time to the pool. Improved quality of instructional time and minimized disruptions to the team's ongoing program resulted.

The two examples above are representative of one level of change that can be made by teams. However, there are more significant second-level changes—in curriculum and instruction—that can and should be made by a team seeking to take advantage of the block. Indeed, planning and conducting interdisciplinary units have been, from the beginning of the middle school movement, an assumed goal of teams. A common requirement has been to have teams do one or two interdisciplinary units annually. Then there are possible team projects that might involve service learning and thematic units organized around a concept and not tied to a particular subject. Teams can arrange for one teacher to work for a short period with a few students needing tutorial assistance. The imagination, creativity, and willingness of teachers to step outside the traditional approaches are the only limits to ways the longer block can be used.

Although teachers may be technically empowered to make decisions regarding the use of time or instructional strategies, unless there is trust between the principal and teachers, few changes will be made. A principal in suburban Detroit described the importance of trust: "I want my teachers to try new things, to take instructional risks. Not everything will work exactly the way we want. I don't second-guess their action. But if it doesn't work or isn't effective, the expectation is that you'll learn from the experience and try something else." Trust is an integral component of schools where teachers are empowered to view time as a resource.

Concluding thoughts

Successful middle level schools readily examine their practices and make adjustments as needed. They have no hesitancy in challenging the norms of traditional practice and assessing every aspect of their programs with the goal of more effectively serving the young adolescent learner. The middle school movement has led to the examination of the use of time and structure as variables that can significantly impact the quality of the program. Using a range of organizational arrangements, empowered teachers have made decisions regarding the use of time and modified curricular and instructional practices that improved student learning.

References

Carroll, J. M. (1989). *The Copernican plan: Restructuring the American high school.* Andover, MA: The Regional Laboratory for Educational Improvement of the Northeast and the Islands.

Edwards, C. M. (1993). Virginia's 4 X 4 high schools: High school, college and more. *NASSP Bulletin, 79*(571), 23-41.

Hackmann, D. G. (1995). Improving the middle school climate: Alternating-day block schedule. *Schools in the Middle, 5*(1), 28-34.

Lipsitz, J. (1984). *Successful schools for young adolescents.* New York: Transaction Books.

McEwin, K., Dickinson, T., & Jenkins, D. (2004). *America's middle schools in the new century: Status and progress.* Westerville, OH: National Middle School Association.

National Middle School Association. (2003). *This we believe: Successful schools for young adolescents.* Westerville, OH: Author.

Valentine, J., Clark, D., Hackmann, D., & Petzko, V. (2002). *A national study of leadership in middle level schools: Volume 1. A national study of middle level leaders and school programs.* Reston, VA: National Association of Secondary School Principals.

Williamson, R. (1998). *Scheduling middle level schools: Tools for improved student achievement.* Reston, VA: National Association of Secondary School Principals.

4

Organizing Time in Various Ways

Creating a flexible schedule may at first seem to be an oxymoron, because the word *schedule* implies a regular, fixed pattern for using time; while *flexible* implies many options. Flexibility in a schedule is as much an attitude as a concept. Ideally, all teachers should have full control over the use of time as they seek to guide the learning of students. But absolute flexibility disappeared with the demise of the one-room schoolhouse. Today's middle schools are large, regularly exceeding 1,000 students, and organizing and managing them involves many factors that help to determine how much flexibility is possible in a schedule.

This chapter introduces several models of organization; some provide greater flexibility than others, but each has advantages and disadvantages. Each one should be viewed as a tool that provides teachers with some blocks of time they can modify to make a quality educational experience for their students. Such flexibility permits them to vary the routine, to match the allocation of time with a particular instructional task, and to work collaboratively across content areas.

Examples of schedules that flex

At one midwestern middle school, each team had a four-period block, either in the morning or the afternoon. Teams routinely altered the allocation of time among the different subjects. Blocks of 100 minutes, rather than the normal 50-minute periods, were established when needed by any one of the teachers. The other teachers on those days adjusted their schedules but found this was not a problem.

Another middle school team with a long instructional block found that among its students, some were more attentive in the morning, others in the afternoon. After team meetings about this topic, they decided to rotate the order of classes each month. This proved to be satisfactory to all, and teachers became aware of how they taught and responded differently at different times of the day.

These are two examples of simple, first-level changes that teachers can make when they have control over the use of time. More imaginative uses of the flexibility will evolve as professional teachers take the initiative.

While there are a number of different approaches to making school time more responsive, we will discuss these: block schedules, alternating day schedules, rotating schedules, dropped schedules, and trimester schedules. Examples will be presented briefly with some advantages and disadvantages noted.

Not surprisingly, the variations on each of the models are numerous, and the approaches may be combined so that a school might have an alternating day block schedule or a rotating trimester schedule. The examples that follow should provoke purposeful conversation in your school about how time can be used to improve the instructional experience of students.

Definition of terms

Before describing alternatives to the traditional, fixed-length period schedule, basic definitions for each of the options described are presented.

Block schedule: Two or more consecutive periods under the direction of a teacher or team that can alter the way time is used.

Alternating day schedule: The entire schedule, or a portion of it, meets every other day. Some models include four long classes one day ("A") and four different long classes on the alternate day ("B").

Rotating schedule: The entire schedule or a portion of it rotates during the day. Most commonly, the class meeting first period on the first day moves to the end of the day on the next day, and other classes rotate up the schedule. The rotation continues so that every class rotates through the day.

Modified block: A version of the block schedule with every class meeting on some days and longer blocks meeting on other days. Another version might include several long blocks and several single period classes meeting on the same day.

Dropped schedule: One or more classes are "dropped" from the schedule on selected days, and some other class or activity replaces the "dropped" class in the schedule.

Parallel block: A group of students is divided into subgroups shared by the teachers; each subgroup meets with a teacher for one or more subjects before the subgroups switch teachers for a different subject or two.

Trimester schedule: The school year is divided into three units rather than the more traditional two semesters or four quarters.

Block schedules and models

By far, the most common flexible schedule is the block schedule. It is closely linked to teaching teams. When the school is organized by teams who have a common schedule and common planning time, the block schedule provides the team opportunities to use the longer period of time as it sees fit. Its general advantages have already been noted. One would be hard-pressed to cite theoretical disadvantages. However, if the block is not effectively used to break away from the usual teacher-directed passive learning approach, it is of little value.

Example 1: Block schedule. One school in the Southwest has a six-period day with four of the periods used for the core subjects. One team has students for these classes during first, second, fifth, and sixth period. Each class is 50 minutes long, so the team has two 100-minute blocks each day, one in the morning and one in the afternoon. The team's schedule is the same every day of the week. Thus over the week the team has ten 100-minute instructional blocks. Each week, during a team meeting, the team talks about instructional activities in each of the classes and decides how they will use their time. Often, each class meets for its usual 50-minute period, but frequently the schedule is altered to provide longer blocks of time for one or more classes. This model is very common, probably found more often than any other except where a team's block is all in one piece, morning or afternoon.

PERIOD	Mon	Tue	Wed	Thu	Fri
1	BLOCK	BLOCK	BLOCK	BLOCK	BLOCK
2					
3	3	3	3	3	3
4	4	4	4	4	4
5	BLOCK	BLOCK	BLOCK	BLOCK	BLOCK
6					

Example 2: Block schedule with length of block varying among grades. This model comes from a middle school in Michigan with a seven-period day, with five of the seven periods included in the block. Students have two exploratory classes daily; lunch is not shown on the following schedule.

Academic blocks are provided throughout the day, but the length of them varies from grade to grade. Sixth graders have a long block early in the day and return to their team teachers for one period at the end of the day. The teachers requested this approach with sixth graders so that they could check with their students about homework and be debriefed at the end of the day.

The school also has a short advisory time at the beginning of the day, which allows students to begin their day with their adviser.

PERIOD	Sixth Grade	Seventh Grade	Eighth Grade
	Advocacy	Advocacy	Advocacy
1	BLOCK	EXPLORATORY	BLOCK
2	BLOCK	BLOCK	BLOCK
3	BLOCK	BLOCK	EXPLORATORY
4	BLOCK	EXPLORATORY	BLOCK
5	EXPLORATORY	BLOCK	BLOCK
6	EXPLORATORY	BLOCK	BLOCK
7	BLOCK	BLOCK	EXPLORATORY

Example 3: Modified block schedule. The school using this schedule is composed of three small houses with teaching teams. One house includes all sixth graders and the other two houses, Maize and Blue (school colors), include both seventh and eighth graders. It also provides long instructional blocks throughout the day as well as opportunities for cross-graded elective classes. Cross-graded electives were important for performing music classes

offered to seventh and eighth graders. There are eight periods each day, and seventh and eighth graders have three electives, while sixth graders have two exploratory classes.

One unique aspect of this schedule is that Maize House and Blue House have variations in the morning schedules as electives may be cross-graded and individually selected. During the afternoon all seventh graders, regardless of house, follow one schedule. All eighth graders, regardless of house, follow another schedule. This provides an opportunity for scheduling classes offered for only a single grade. It also allows students to have lunch with their grade-specific group, an important consideration for students in this school.

House Grade 6	Maize House Grades 7/8	Blue House Grades 7/8
	ELECTIVE	ELECTIVE
BLOCK	BLOCK	BLOCK
LUNCH	ELECTIVE	ELECTIVE
	ALL 7TH GRADERS AFTERNOON	ALL 8TH GRADERS AFTERNOON
BLOCK	LUNCH	ELECTIVE
	BLOCK	LUNCH
EXPLORATORY		BLOCK
EXPLORATORY	ELECTIVE	

Example 4: Modules. The goal of the faculty at this Ohio school was to provide blocks as long as possible for core teams and a block for exploratory teachers. The school day was 390 minutes long, divided into 13 modules of 30 minutes. One module was allotted for lunch, three for exploratory classes, and nine for core classes.

The final schedule provided a three-period block for exploratory teachers with common planning time during the fourth and fifth module. Each teacher could choose to vary the time used for individual exploratory classes.

Core teams were provided two long instructional blocks, one in the morning and the other in the afternoon, during which time they could employ varied activities and capitalize on connections between subjects.

	Sixth Grade	Seventh Grade	Eighth Grade
1	Core (150 minutes)		Exploratory (90 minutes)
2	Core (150 minutes)		Exploratory (90 minutes)
3	Core (150 minutes)	Core (180 minutes)	Exploratory (90 minutes)
4	Core (150 minutes)	Core (180 minutes)	
5	Core (150 minutes)	Core (180 minutes)	Core (120 minutes)
6	Lunch	Core (180 minutes)	Core (120 minutes)
7	Lunch	Core (180 minutes)	Core (120 minutes)
8	Core (120 minutes)	Lunch	Lunch
9	Core (120 minutes)	Exploratory (90 minutes)	Lunch
10	Core (120 minutes)	Exploratory (90 minutes)	Core (150 minutes)
11	Exploratory (90 minutes)	Core (90 minutes)	Core (150 minutes)
12	Exploratory (90 minutes)	Core (90 minutes)	Core (150 minutes)
13	Exploratory (90 minutes)	Core (90 minutes)	Core (150 minutes)

Alternating day schedules

A second type of schedule is the alternating day schedule. The most common version is referred to as a 4 x 4 block schedule. This model, used widely in high schools, provides four classes a 90-minute block on one day, while four other classes meet for an extended block on the alternate day. The classes alternate every other day all year long. Below is a general alternating day block schedule (numbers refer to classes).

	Mon	Tue	Wed	Thu	Fri
8:00 – 9:30 a.m.	1	5	1	5	1
9:35 – 11:05 a.m.	2	6	2	6	2
11:45 a.m.– 1:15 p.m.	3	7	3	7	3
1:20 – 2:50 p.m.	4	8	4	8	4

Example 5: Alternating day block schedule. A Texas school that wanted to provide long instructional blocks for its teaching teams adopted this version of an alternating day block schedule. Four classes meet each day using an odd-even day schedule.

This example from one sixth grade team includes language arts and algebra prep for an extended block each day. Social studies and science meet for an extended block every other day, with two different exploratory classes on alternate days. The schedule doubled the time allocated to language arts and mathematics, reflecting the current concern with low math scores and reading levels. Ninety minute blocks every day were twice as long as the daily 45-minute class periods provided in their earlier schedule.

A 90-minute block on alternate days provides the same number of minutes for instruction as a class meeting 45 minutes daily. The advantage of this model is that every time a class meets, it meets for an extended class period. A disadvantage is that every class does not meet every day, and at least for some students, forgetting content between meeting days may be an issue.

Example 6: Alternating semester block schedule. This variation of an alternating schedule was adopted by a south Texas school. Three 90-minute blocks meet each day along with two 45-minute classes for exploratory

(Example 5)

Odd Day	Even Day
Advisory (25 minutes)	Advisory (25 minutes)
Language Arts (90 minutes)	Language Arts (90 minutes)
Algebra Prep (90 minutes)	Algebra Prep (90 minutes)
Lunch	Lunch
Social Studies (90 minutes)	Science (90 minutes)
Exploratory #1 (90 minutes)	Exploratory #2 (90 minutes)

subjects. As in Example 5, this sixth grade schedule for one team, language arts and mathematics, meets for an extended block each day throughout the year. Social studies and science, however, meet for a 90-minute block daily for one semester. Students have one subject in the first semester and the other during second semester. From the standpoint of the middle school concept, this practice is of questionable validity since social studies and science are equally important in the education of a young adolescent, but it is now commonly used as a result of accountability testing.

Example 7: Modified alternating day schedule. This example provides a variation on the alternating schedules used in examples 5 and 6. In this schedule, every class meets three times each week with two long instructional blocks and one shorter class period. Four of the eight classes meet every day but Wednesday. On Wednesday every class meets. It does not seem to have a distinctive advantage but is an option (numbers refer to classes).

Example 8: Modified alternating day schedule. Another variation of the alternating day format is shown in this schedule. The staff wanted to be sure

(Example 6)

	Semester 1	Semester 2
1 2	Language Arts (90 minutes)	Language Arts (90 minutes)
3 4	Mathematics (90 minutes)	Mathematics (90 minutes)
	Lunch	Lunch
5 6	Social Studies (90 minutes)	Science (90 minutes)
7	Exploratory #1 (45 minutes)	Exploratory #3 (45 minutes)
8	Exploratory #2 (45 minutes)	Exploratory #4 (45 minutes)

(Example 7)

Mon	Tue	Wed	Thu	Fri
1	5	1	1	5
		2		
2	6	3	2	6
		4		
3	7	5	3	7
		6		
4	8	7	4	8
		8		

that each class had both long instructional blocks and met several times each week to ensure continuity of instruction. Thus every class meets four days each week.

Rotating schedules

The name describes what a rotating schedule does when all or some of the schedule literally rotates from day to day or week to week. Classes meet at

(Example 8)

Mon	Tue	Wed	Thu	Fri
1	1	1	5	1
2		2		2
3	2	3	6	3
4		4		4
5	3	5	7	5
6		6		6
7	4	7	8	7
8		8		8

different times on different days. The prime and perhaps only advantage of the rotating schedule is that it allows students and teachers to work with one another at different times of the day, providing an equal opportunity for all classes to work when students presumably are at their best or their worst. This schedule does not give teachers a longer block.

Example 9: Rotating schedule. The entire schedule, or a portion of the schedule, rotates during the day in this model. Most commonly the class meeting first period on the first day moves to the end of the day on the next day and other classes rotate up the schedule. The rotation continues so that every class rotates through the schedule (numbers refer to classes).

Mon		Tues		Wed		Thu		Fri
1		2		3		4		5
2		3		4		5		6
3		4		5		6		1
4		5		6		1		2
5		6		1		2		3
6		1		2		3		4

Example 10: Modified rotating schedule. Another example of a rotating schedule is to rotate seven or eight classes through a six or seven period day. For example in a seven period rotation, only six of the seven classes meet on any given day.

Day	Periods
1	Periods 1-6
2	Periods 2-7
3	Periods 3-1
4	Periods 4-2
5	Periods 5-3
6	Periods 6-4
7	Periods 7-5

The schedule might look something like this:

Mon	Tues	Wed	Thu	Fri
1	2	3	4	5
2	3	4	5	6
3	4	5	6	7
4	5	6	7	1
5	6	7	1	2
6	7	1	2	3

Example 11: Rotating schedule within a team block. Rotation can also be used within a large instructional block. One team in Michigan noticed what other teams had that their students responded differently depending on the time of the day. The team had a four-period instructional block and decided to rotate the order the classes met every quarter.

As a result of adopting their rotating schedule the team reported that they recognized the differences among students based on when each class met and that overall, they had a more balanced appreciation for the strengths of their students. This model however, is useful only when the four teachers maintain their separate, departmentalized teaching.

Example 12: Modified rotating block schedule. This example is used in a British Columbia middle school. This eighth grade schedule illustrates the rotation of eight classes over a five-day week. Students have one teacher for a two-period humanities (language arts and social studies) block and another teacher for the two-period science and math block. Most classes meet four days per week; but two of the exploratory classes, physical education and technology-computers, meet only three days.

Mon	Tues	Wed	Thu	Fri
1	7	5	3	1
2	8	6	4	2
3	1	7	5	3
4	2	8	6	4
5	3	1	7	5
6	4	2	8	6

KEY

1 & 2 – Humanities (E/SS)

3 & 4 – Science/Math

5 – Band

6 – French

7 – PE

Dropped schedules

In this plan one or more classes are dropped from the schedule on selected days, and another class or activity replaces the dropped class. While each of the regular classes loses one class period occasionally, it provides a period that can be used for many activities and doesn't otherwise complicate the schedule.

Example 13: Dropped schedule. Here a class is dropped each Tuesday and Thursday to provide a time for student activities, clubs, intramural sports, or an advisory class.

(Example 13)

Mon	Tue	Wed	Thu	Fri
1	1	1	1	1
2	Activity	2	2	2
3	3	3	3	3
4	4	4	4	4
5	5	5	Activity	5
6	6	6	6	6

Example 14: Modified dropped schedule. This example comes from a school in western Michigan. Most core classes (language arts, science, social studies, and physical education) meet four days per week, but mathematics meets five days. "Dropping" the four core classes one period a day from Tuesday through Friday opens a spot in the schedule to add mini-courses. The mini-courses meet at the end of the day and provide an opportunity for students to select an area of interest. Some students, however, may be required to take specific mini-courses that provide additional instruction in areas in which they need assistance. All student clubs and student government meet at this time.

Periods	1	2	3	4	5	6	7
Mon	M	U	SS		S	P	LA
Tue	M	U	SS		S	P	MC
Wed	LA	M	U	L U N	SS	S	MC
Thu	P	LA	M	C H	U	SS	MC
Fri	S	P	LA		M	U	MC

LA	Language Arts	S	Science
M	Mathematics	SS	Social Studies
MC	Mini-Courses	U	Unified Arts (Art, Family
P	Physical Education		Living, Music, Lab, Technology)

Trimester schedules

This model divides the school year into three units—fall, winter, and spring. The schedule provides some of the benefits of longer instructional blocks found in a block schedule and may provide additional classes for students.

Example 15: Trimester schedule. This schedule comes from a school in Massachusetts that was looking for a way to continue teaming and provide common planning time for teams.

The staff was interested in offering fewer classes each day with each class meeting for a longer period of time. They were also interested in continuing to provide students with rich exploratory class experiences.

The previous schedule had seven classes each day with teachers teaching six of the seven. Maintaining the same length for the school day but reducing the number of classes to six increased the length of each from 42 minutes to 55 minutes. Teachers would teach five of the six classes.

In order to maintain desired exploratory offerings, the school year was divided into trimesters rather than the traditional semesters. Thus students had six trimesters of exploratory classes rather than four semesters of classes. Some classes met for a single trimester, others like foreign language or performing music met for all three trimesters.

This schedule from a single grade shows that a student might have four core classes and two exploratory classes each trimester. In this example choir meets each of the trimesters while the other exploratory classes meet for a single trimester.

Period	Fall	Winter	Spring
1	Math	Math	Math
2	Science	Science	Science
3	Geography	Geography	Geography
4	ELA	ELA	ELA
5	PE	Art	Tech
6	Choir	Choir	Choir

Example 16. Trimester schedule with blocks. This schedule was designed for a rural school in western Michigan. The number of classes each day was reduced from six to five thus lengthening each class. Teachers teach four

of the five periods. This design was selected to provide each student with additional time in language arts and mathematics. This was accomplished by lengthening each class period while reducing the number of daily classes from six to five. So that students could still have more than one exploratory class, science and social studies met only two of the three trimesters. The school has teams that have common planning time when students are at exploratory classes. This example from a single grade shows a typical student's schedule.

Period	Fall	Winter	Spring
1	Lang Arts	Lang Arts	Lang Arts
2	Math	Math	Math
3	Exploratory	Exploratory	Exploratory
4	Science	Science	Exploratory
5	Exploratory	Soc Studies	Soc Studies

Concluding thoughts

In this chapter, we identified and illustrated some common ways that the schedule could be altered to provide the flexibility teams want so they could use various instructional strategies that were difficult if not impossible to carry out in a single 45–50-minute period. The widespread existence of interdisciplinary teams, with their inherent commitment to fostering connections between subjects, made flexibility a priority and led to the development of longer instructional blocks.

The block time arrangements provided here all started with the traditional schedule of uniform periods for subjects, and that schedule is maintained apart from the combining of two or more periods in some fashion on some occasions to create blocks of time. The schedule alterations themselves don't mandate any changes in practice; they only provide opportunities for teams to engage—if they so desire—in deviations from the separate subject approach that predominates in American education.

In the next chapters, some organizing and scheduling models that do not start with the assumption of periods for subjects are considered. These models involve increased participation by the students in their education.

5

Using Time More Creatively

A number of other more progressive organizational models have emerged in middle schools. They are not new; in fact, they reflect the days of the one- and two-room school and the progressive era of the 30s. These models all are developmentally responsive and provide teachers with flexibility in time use. While they are not yet common, these practices have proven most effective in meeting both the academic achievement and the developmental responsibilities of middle level education. They are certain to be found in more and more middle level schools in the years ahead.

Partner teams

A relatively simple model that has become more widespread is the two-person or partner team. The four-person interdisciplinary team has become somewhat the standard and is still the likely goal of the limited number of middle level schools that have not yet committed to teaming. However, the limitations of large teams become obvious when teachers seek to implement more fully recommended middle school practices—particularly curriculum integration. Departmentalization has a way of perpetuating itself when teams are comprised of teachers representing specific disciplines.

Another factor supporting partner teams has been the need to reduce the stress students feel when transitioning from self-contained fifth grade classes to a situation where they have seven or eight different teachers. To make the transition smoother and then carry it forward, some schools have established two-person teams at the entry level, three-person teams at the seventh grade level, and in preparation for the high school's departmentalization, four-person teams at the eighth grade level. Many schools offer two-person teams as an option, usually at the sixth grade level. Chris Stevenson, a strong advocate for small teams, has offered these statements in support of partner teams.

The modifier of partner deserves special attention when used to describe a team. The key element in such teams is the achievement of partnership—a collaboration that involves the three central constituencies in every school: teachers, students, parents. The essential partnership that must be formed from the very beginning concerns the two teachers who work closely together to invent and sustain the educational program for the team. A second dimension of partnership is between the teachers and their students; exemplary teams are true communities of adults and children in which students have an active voice in their education. The third partnership is between the two adult constituencies—teachers and parents. When teachers and parents work well together, the children who are the objects of their efforts also thrive.

(Bishop, & Allen-Malley, 2004, p. viii)

Partner teams positively impact teaching and learning because of their smallness. When going from a four-person team with more than 100 students to a two-person team, you cut the number of students in half and work with those fewer students for twice as long! This change alone is significant, as it increases teachers' knowledge about and understanding of individual students, and student-teacher relationships deepen. Depending on the school's schedule, partner teams may have one long block, two smaller ones, or a three-one split; but however their instructional time is set, the teachers can control how it is used.

A growing body of literature supports smaller teams, both in terms of academic effectiveness and teacher satisfaction, as well as earning the full endorsement of parents. Flowers, Mertens, and Mulhall (2000) summarized longitudinal data from 70 middle schools and concluded "Clearly smaller teams are better able to manage not only the team coordination that is necessary for best practice, but also the classroom practices that serve to implement the programs" (p. 56). Small teams magnify the benefits of teaming. Although certification may present a problem for some teachers desiring to implement this practice, it is usually not an issue, as most middle school faculties include teachers holding elementary certification. National Middle School Association's book, *The Power of Two: Partner Teams in Action* (Bishop & Allen-Malley, 2004) allows one to step into the world of eight partner teams, understand how they work, and gain an appreciation for the special advantages and rewards of partner teaming.

Looping

The practice of having a teacher and class stay together for two or more years is a very old practice that has been revived in many elementary schools and in an increasing number of middle schools. Providing long-term student-teacher relationships as children undergo changes in every phase of their being is in itself a justification for looping. More meaningful teacher-parent relationships, the ability to know students' learning styles well, the ease of adapting curriculum and instruction, and being able to work on those critical long-term objectives are other benefits of looping. Looping teachers fashion their own schedules, particularly because they can take advantage of the time gained in the fall when other teachers are getting acquainted with new students and reviewing. Looping teachers usually plan summer activities and projects with students so learning will be ongoing in this otherwise lost time.

The student-teacher progression plan, as looping is sometimes called, just makes good sense and leads one to wonder why it isn't practiced more widely. Students, teachers, and parents in all parts of the country where it is in place always give it high marks (George & Lounsbury, 2000).

Multiage grouping

Multiage grouping is another practice coming back into use, because it fits so well with early adolescence. Technically, every middle school class is multiage, even though organized by presumed chronological likeness; but multiage grouping is an organizational strategy in which students of different ages, grade levels, and abilities are intentionally placed together under the direction of a team for a three-year cycle. As one-third of the group—the eighth graders—moves on to the next level, a new group of sixth graders joins the team with the result that any one student completes a three-year experience with the same teachers. This practice carries the same benefits as looping plus many others. The social aspects of an education are especially well served by the extended interpersonal relationships. Students teach each other, develop friendships, and grow in their respect for others and in their ability to interact effectively with others.

Flexibility in scheduling, as in looping, is very much in the hands of the team members for the extended instructional block they have with their students. While multiage grouping may appear at first to be somewhat radical—although practiced regularly in music and athletics without any reservations—once assumptions based on traditional school organization are set aside, it is seen as an educationally sound and very developmentally appropriate arrangement for achieving all the goals of middle level education.

Perhaps the best-known example is the Alpha Team in Shelburne, Vermont, which has employed this arrangement for more than 30 years (discussed briefly in a subsequent section). The educational advantages of the long-term, student-teacher relationships and the flexibility of curriculum and instruction are so great that where a school has committed teachers interested in a multiage group, successful implementation will be certain.

Schools-within-a-school

A fourth practice that responds to the growing size of schools, which brings impersonality and alienation, is the schools-within-a-school concept. *Turning Points* (Carnegie Corporation, 1989) supported this organizational practice. Under this arrangement, a too-big school of, for example, 1,200 students is subdivided into three schools or houses of 400 students. Each house is a balanced microcosm of the total school. Students remain in the same house, which usually retains the format of grade level teams, all three years with the same faculty and administration for their core curriculum, while mixing with students from the other houses for lunch and exploratories. Various applications of this plan have been practiced for many years in many states. Wakulla Middle School in Florida and Nock Middle School in Massachusetts have operated schools-within-a-school successfully for more than 25 years. The school-within-a-school model may not immediately employ looping or multiage grouping, but both practices can evolve in such schools. The benefits of long-term student-teacher relationships and a more personalized environment are immediately achieved without introducing any new or unfamiliar practices. National Middle School Association's book, *Making Big Schools Feel Small* (George & Lounsbury, 2000) provides a thorough discussion of multiage grouping, looping, and schools-within-a-school with rationale, examples, and research relating to these practices.

Integrated learning models

There are several examples of programs that are even more thoroughly student-centered, practice a very high degree of curriculum integration, and are committed to practicing democracy. In these situations, the schedule could be called a "no-schedule schedule," for there is no schedule of periods in place from which to deviate. Students and teachers collaborate in determining how each day's block will be used. While all the scheduling models discussed earlier were adaptations or adjustments of a schedule basically established to provide time for the core subjects, these models do not start with subjects or periods as factors in determining how time will be used.

The Alpha Team in Shelburne, Vermont, pioneered in establishing what is often considered the best model of the middle school concept fully implemented. The Alpha students—sixth, seventh, and eighth graders under the guidance of three teachers—set their own learning goals and ways to achieve them. They assume responsibility for their education and develop the learning skills and dispositions that equip them to be lifelong learners and democratic citizens. The book, *The Story of Alpha: A Multiage, Student-Centered Team—33 Years and Counting* (Kuntz, 2005) chronicles the inspiring story of the courageous teachers who successfully gave and continue to give life to this significant educational program.

The other notable examples of programs that practice fully integrated curriculum exist in Radnor Middle School in Wayne, Pennsylvania, where teacher Mark Springer and his teaching partner first created and launched in 1987 the seventh grade program Watershed. Every aspect of the curriculum relates to various aspects of life, past and present, that occur in the watershed. No set schedule exists; and no formal classes are taught, no grades are given, and students are the prime decision makers in the block of time the program has been allotted. This program is popular with students and parents and continues in its 21st year with two other teachers. Mark left the program in 1998 to establish an eighth grade program, Soundings. In Soundings, both what is studied and how learning is pursued are determined fully by the students. As with Watershed, Soundings students not only score well on all the various tests of academic achievement but also become critical thinkers who have initiative and well-developed social skills. The details of these powerful programs that engage students so effectively in their own education are provided in the books *Watershed: A Successful Voyage Into Integrative Learning* (Springer, 1994) and *Soundings: A Democratic, Student-Centered Education* (Springer, 2006). These resources not only provide descriptions but also rationales and evidences of success, and they demonstrate how meaningful education can be when the barriers of subjects, periods, and a prescribed curriculum are removed.

Concluding thoughts

Emerging from a myriad of research studies conducted in recent decades, there has come one significant generalization: small is better. There is no way to get around the judgment that smaller schools are more likely to be successful than larger ones. Student attitude and achievement, attendance, participation in activities, teacher satisfaction and sense of efficacy, and parental involvement are among benefits directly associated with smallness. Deborah Meier (as cited in George & Lounsbury, 2000), the highly respected educational innovator in New York City, made this claim:

> Small schools come as close to being a panacea for America's educational ills as we're likely to get. Smallness is a prerequisite for the climate and culture that we need to develop the habits of the heart and mind essential to a democracy. Such a culture emerges from authentic relationships built on face-to-face conversations by people engaged in common work and common work standards. (p. 3)

This sound position comes at a time when schools are getting larger, and there is growing concern among middle level educators over the increasing size of middle schools. All the scheduling and organizational models described in this book are actually responses to this reality. Interdisciplinary teams take a major step toward providing an educational environment of smallness as they work with a common group of students in a longer block to build a sense of family in a learning community where collaboration is prevalent. The models presented in this chapter have moved much farther in achieving smallness, but in every case scheduling is a way to support smaller units that nurture long-term teacher-student relationships and counter the anonymity and alienation that accompany bigness.

References

Bishop, P., & Allen-Malley, G. (2004). *The power of two: Partner teams in action*. Westerville, OH: National Middle School Association.

Carnegie Council on Adolescent Development (1989). *Turning points: Preparing American youth for the 21st Century*. New York: Carnegie Corporation.

George, P., & Lounsbury, J. (2000). *Making big schools feel small: Multiage grouping, looping, and schools-within-a-school*. Westerville, OH: National Middle School Association.

Kuntz, S. (2005). *The story of Alpha: A multiage, student-centered team—33 years and counting*. Westerville, OH: National Middle School Association.

Springer, M. (1994). *Watershed: A successful voyage into integrated learning*. Columbus, OH: National Middle School Association.

Springer, M. (2006). *Soundings: A democratic student-centered education*. Westerville, OH: National Middle School Association.

6

Getting Started

As advanced throughout this book, a school's schedule is critical. It defines the structure of the day, facilitates or inhibits interaction among staff, regulates the instructional program, and reflects the values of the school. Recently, school schedules have come to reflect more directly the current emphasis on accountability by test scores and have likely undergone alteration. Launching a conversation about the school's schedule anytime, however, provokes a variety of responses. Some applaud the initiative; others are hesitant, even opposed, to considering any change, while others adopt a wait-and-see attitude. Given this reality, careful thought and planning must be brought to bear when the time comes to build the schedule.

Strategies for launching the conversation

There are ways to work with the school community when embarking on a revision of the school's schedule. Three approaches will be described and will include several specific techniques that may be used with planning groups.

Strategy 1: Plan for purposeful engagement.

Undertaking any major reform should not be done in isolation. It is essential that school stakeholders be involved in exploring and examining alternatives and in making recommendations. Teachers, of course, must be included when the schedule is under consideration, for they are the ones who will give life to the schedule.

In some communities the parameters of participation may be defined by board of education policy or by the collective bargaining agreement. Previous practice may call for a faculty committee to be appointed to work with the administration in developing a new schedule. Quite often in days past, while groups or individuals may have been invited to offer suggestions, the actual development of the schedule was viewed as an administrative responsibility. In any case, there is a history in the district that has to be considered.

Regardless of the approach used, there are some things to consider when identifying various individuals who will be involved in some way in revising the schedule. The following five could serve as guidelines.

- Communicate in advance the process that will be used in selecting members to participate in revising the schedule.
- Assure representative membership.
- Ensure participation by those with the most to lose or gain.
- Involve some who are "known dissenters."
- Include members who can contribute specific expertise.

Tool A. Start the conversation around current conditions.

Purpose: Develop a shared context for the discussion.

1. Individual faculty members are asked to identify and make notes including evidence of problems with the current schedule.

2. In teams of two or three, teachers discuss the problems they identified, reach consensus on a ranking for their group on major concerns, cite evidence, and note implications for the school on a chart.

Concern	Evidence	Implications

Strategy 2: Assure a common base of information

Members of any collaborative group bring their personal knowledge and expertise to the conversation. There are usually substantial differences in perceptions between members from internal groups (teachers, administrators) and those from external groups (parents, community) that have to be considered. To launch a meaningful conversation, then, it is important to have a common base of information about the topic. For example, everyone in the group might read a set of articles about the topic or review a shared set of data about student performance. In a suburban Chicago district the study group agreed that no member would cite "research" without providing a copy of the research—an article, an abstract, or a full citation. This strategy helped to minimize members' portraying themselves as experts on the topic.

It is also helpful to identify the varied perspectives on an issue. Tool B provides a format for focusing on "evidence" and areas of agreement and disagreement. A conversation about the varied perspectives can contribute to a better understanding of the issues and their implications.

Tool B. Identify varied perspectives.

Issue:_____

Evidence "Group A" uses	Evidence "Group B" uses
Areas of Agreement	**Areas of Disagreement**

It is important to gather and then use data when making decisions. Many study groups find it useful to identify and gather the data they need and spend time working together noting patterns and trends.

Schools possess lots of readily available data about student learning, school climate, and curricular and instructional processes. Types of data that might be collected and used are identified in Tool C.

Tool C. Gather and use various forms of data.

Type of Data	Examples
• Readily available data	• Student attendance • Student test scores • Student course selection information • School climate surveys • Current allocation of time
• Create data	• Shadow students to get information about the school day from their perspectives. • Conduct a focus group discussion with a group of parents or students. • Administer a short survey to students, parents, and staff.
• Artifacts and student work	• Examine examples of student work. • Present graphically ways that time is currently utilized. • Examine copies of the current schedule to identify patterns that might be continued or are in need of modification.

Strategy 3. Be clear about the process.

Many groups flounder because they fail to spend time talking about and agreeing on the processes that the group will use for both operations and decision making. Often there is resistance to devoting valuable work group time on process details. However, these conversations are invaluable when the group begins to deal with difficult and contentious issues. Using the following norms of operation and collaboration can facilitate clarifying how the group will operate and make decisions.

Operation
  • Start and end each meeting on time.
  • Provide a written agenda prior to each meeting.
  • Provide time to reflect and think about the process.
  • Gather missed information after an absence.
  • Provide all information and minutes to the entire committee even if the information pertains to only an individual or a subcommittee.
  • Provide a communiqué to all stakeholders following each meeting.

Collaboration
- Remain focused on students' best interests.
- Demonstrate respect in all verbal and non-verbal communication.
- Give equal consideration to all ideas and concerns.
- Keep all issues and conflicts within the room.
- Voice all questions and disagreements.
- Avoid personalizing issues.
- Provide rationale and other support for all opinions.
- Use consensus for decision making.

Tool D. *Achieving agreement on norms of operation and collaboration.*

Step 1: In groups of three, talk about norms of operation that you would like this group to follow.

Step 2: Share the ideas from the groups using a round-robin reporting system to see what norms of operation seem to emerge. Build a list of most frequently selected norms.

Step 3: In small groups, review the list of norms of collaboration and identify three norms that your group feels are most critical to the group's work.

Step 4: Share these norms with the total group and reach agreement on the ones the group will accept for their study.

One school established the following format for sharing and reporting recommendations.

1. *Statement of the issue*: Describe the problem or issue being discussed and the data or information that indicate it is an issue.

2. *Objectives*: State the objectives to be achieved in addressing the problem or issue.

3. *Process used to develop alternatives*: Describe the constituent groups who participated in the process used to develop the issues analysis and generate the alternatives and recommendation.

4. *Alternatives considered*: Provide a description of the various alternatives considered including the advantages and disadvantages of each.

5. *Recommended alternative*: Decide on the preferred alternative and provide detail about the rationale for its recommendation.

6. *Evaluation*: Provide a process for measuring the effectiveness of the recommended alternative including indicators or measures of effectiveness, ideas for data collection, and time line.

7. *Procedures and time line for implementation*: Include a time line for finalizing a decision on the alternative and a time line for implementation.

Tool E. Decision-making options.

Each of the following ways to make decisions has some merit and some disadvantages. What is most critical is that the faculty select a process *prior* to the presentation of any scheduling options.

Option	Brief Description
1. Vote with majority prevailing	Occasionally a secret ballot is used. Generally, an issue is discussed until at least half of the group members arrive at a decision they can support. Works best when opportunity has been provided for open discussion of all points of view.
1A. A vote with super-majority required (66% or 75%)	This option assures a substantial majority supports the alternative.
2. Consensus	The issue is discussed until a general agreement on something everyone can support has emerged. Be careful about "false consensus," which may occur if members fail to speak up. This can happen due to time pressure, fatigue, peer pressure, confusion, or complexity of the issue.
3. Fist of Five	Participants raise their hands and show the level of their support by the number of fingers raised (from 0 to 5). Agreement is required on minimum number of fingers needed from each participant. For example, everyone has at least 3 fingers raised.
4. Consensogram	A variation of the "fist of five." Participants indicate their level of support by percentage. Agreement might require everyone to be at least 70% supportive. A variation that provides a bit more secrecy of one's vote is to use sticky notes and a chart listing the various percentages. The completed chart provides a visual indicator of support.

Consensus is usually the preferred decision-making norm; occasionally, it fails. In that case it is necessary to have a plan

One school in northern Illinois made the following statement about how to proceed if consensus failed.

> If consensus fails, seek additional information by
> - Clarifying the position of the participant(s) who cannot consent.
> - Gathering additional information (e.g., research, surveys).
> - Considering the opinion of an outside consultant.
>
> You can also redesign or restructure the proposal by
> - Identifying alternatives.
> - Elaborating more fully the advantages and disadvantages of each alternative.
>
> Then seek consensus again by
> - Considering mediation by an outside consultant.

It is also useful to adopt processes that facilitate the group's work. Tool F lists some procedures that work groups have found useful.

Tool F. Possible group procedures guides.

Ground rules to facilitate group work:
- Have a prepared agenda for each meeting.
- Prepare minutes from each meeting and distribute prior to the next one.
- Follow an informal version of *Robert's Rules of Order*.
- Define a quorum.
- Agree on items at meetings other than the ones in which they are introduced, unless they are emergencies.
- Utilize consensus for decision making.
- Provide for recording and distributing minority reports or dissenting opinions if consensus cannot be reached.

Guidelines for being a helpful group member:
- Arrive on time for meetings.
- Read information prior to the meeting.
- Assume responsibility with others for the well-being of the group.
- Ask clarifying questions.
- Have a positive attitude about the group's work.
- Support other group members.
- Share your knowledge and expertise.

Coping with resistance

One of the challenges to address is resistance of staff or community members to a school improvement initiative. Often resistance is derived from prior experiences that may be completely unrelated to the current initiative. Because dissent is usually based on feelings and beliefs rather than information or data, it is often difficult to address. Those in leadership positions can help groups deal with resistance by facilitating a process for clarifying feelings and allowing the dissenters to work through their concerns. This reinforces the recognition that schools are human enterprises and the human factor must be taken into account during any reform activity.

Resistance usually emerges from several areas. They include the lack of a compelling rationale for the change, a failure to involve others in studying the issue and offering recommendations, the lack of a widely held vision for the school, cynicism about past initiatives never fully implemented, and a belief that the decision has already been made by those in positions of authority.

Ignoring resistance is counterproductive. Pretending that there is no resistance simply provides the dissenters with another issue—not being listened to. An alternative is to treat dissent as rational. Legitimize it and turn it into an advantage. Discuss the issues with individuals and groups. Listen for the central or key issue. Ask clarifying questions. Use neutral, non-inflammatory language. Remember that dissent is based on feelings, beliefs, and individual perceptions, even when concerns may be inaccurate or illogical. Don't take criticism personally and make a good faith effort to respond to all questions and deal with the issues.

One helpful strategy is to ask people to write out their comments or questions. Committing their thoughts to paper will provide an opportunity to lessen some of the emotion and provide a way to gather constituent input. It further helps to identify the specific information needs of those attending the meeting.

Another strategy is to involve known dissenters in the planning process. It is much more difficult to criticize a plan when you have been included in developing it. Involving dissenters may not stifle dissent but will provide a legitimate forum for allowing them to share their concerns.

Planning the process

Frequently, when a school launches a discussion about changing its schedule, a small work group studies the issues and makes preliminary recommendations. Teachers and other school personnel generally constitute most of the group but occasionally parents and other community members may be involved. When beginning such a study, attention to the following items will facilitate the process:

1. *Clearly define the task and establish a time line.* Be explicit about the charge to the work group. Groups function best when the task is clear, specific, and time bound. For example, rather than ask the group to "study how to improve the schedule," the group might be asked to "identify the areas of concern with the current schedule, investigate alternatives, and make a recommendation no later than January 30."

2. *Clarify values and priorities.* Identifying priorities is essential when several important elements compete for time. Tensions likely will arise as competing values are discussed. Being clear about priorities and the underlying values helps to clarify the task of consideration of scheduling alternatives.

One Illinois district developed these statements of rationale and priorities to guide its scheduling process.

- We believe in a more flexible and efficient use of time to better meet student needs.
- Incorporating blocks of time facilitates flexibility in time and integration of curriculum.
- Block scheduling allows for the flexibility, daily contact, team planning, integration, and more continuity needed by the middle level student.
- Our shared understanding places importance on the value of flexibility that blocks of time provide. Larger chunks of time also provide more efficiency. The larger block increases the probability of accommodating individual needs and is less stressful for students and staff. Daily contact is also important.
- A desirable schedule would provide flexibility, daily contact (although not necessarily equal time), and longer periods of instructional time, while maintaining the high quality of instruction currently offered.

3. *Frame the conversation around critical questions.* A useful strategy for launching a conversation about the use of time is to frame it around several questions. Questions provide an opportunity to examine varying points of

view and to discuss issues that are often contentious. Several study groups used the following questions to frame their work.

- *Choice:* Do students have any choices in their curricular program? If so, what is the appropriate balance between required courses and elective courses?
- *Instructional block:* What options exist for blocks? What are the implications for teaching and learning?
- *Integration:* Are there curricular areas that no longer offer separate and distinct courses? If so, what are they? How might they be integrated into other curricular areas?
- *Time:* Do all classes need the same amount of time? Do all class periods need to be of equal length? If not, how might they differ? What might be the appropriate allocation of time for each class?
- *Value:* Are some subjects more important than others? If so, how does this importance manifest itself in the school schedule?

Concluding thoughts

Launching a conversation about changing a school's schedule may be contentious, because scheduling is an explicit expression of a school's priorities and values. Modifying the schedule often reflects a change in priorities; and even though the changes are appropriate because of changing conditions, the changes provoke passionate feelings among stakeholders.

Paying close attention to the processes used to conduct such a study can minimize the divisiveness and protectiveness that changing the schedule may provoke. If all the stakeholders in a discussion about the schedule can keep in mind that, at its most fundamental level, the schedule is a tool for transmitting their agreed-upon values and norms, a successful plan for a quality education can result.

Postscript

Teachers and principals face an ever-expanding set of expectations for greater accountability and improved student learning. It is easy to become focused on the latest test scores and curricular standards and not see that the schedule itself may be handicapping efforts to meet accountability standards.

The school's schedule is a fundamental and powerful tool for shaping the instructional program. It can facilitate sound, high-quality instructional practices that will improve student achievement—or stand in the way.

In every example of how a school organized time included in this book, the schedule served a specific purpose of that faculty, but had its limitations and disadvantages. In scheduling, so many factors come into play—conflicting priorities, the pressure to improve students' scores, the desire to expand curricular options, support for continuing well-accepted practices, and the always present need to reduce costs—that some important and worthy programs will inevitably be denied all the time they desire.

The schedule is very much a public display of a school's priorities and values. Changing it calls for special people who are willing to challenge long-standing norms and revisit and reexamine those underlying beliefs or assumptions that initially guided the schedule's development. Because the schedule impacts the everyday routines of school life, conversations about it provoke debate. The most successful efforts emerge when the voices of all interested parties are heard, when ample time is provided for dialogue, when respect for others' points of view is present, where improving the educational experiences of students is kept as the most important consideration, and where consensus is reached.

I hope you will find the examples and the tools described in this text helpful. They reflect what has worked for scheduling for many teachers and principals throughout the nation. I would enjoy the chance to learn from you about ways that you have modified your school's schedule to positively impact student learning. My e-mail address is rwmson214@aol.com.

Thank you for your willingness to consider embarking on the courageous journey of improving your students' education.   —RW